From High School to College

Boarding Pass to Success

Gustavo Gac-Artigas

Translator & Editor:
Dr. Priscilla Gac-Artigas

Ediciones Nuevo Espacio
Second Edition, July 2004

Boarding Pass to Success
Copyright © Gustavo Gac-Artigas
All rights reserved.
No part of this publication may be reproduced, stored in a retrieval system, or transmitted, in any form or by any means (electronic, mechanical, photocopying, recording or otherwise), without the prior written permission of both, the copyright owner and the publisher of this book.
Ediciones Nuevo Espacio
New Jersey, 07704, USA
http://www.editorial-ene.com
ednuevoespacio@aol.com
Editor & Translator: Dr. Priscilla Gac-Artigas
First Edition, March 2004
Second Edition, July 2004
ISBN: 1-930879-38-5

To my people,
those who dare to believe in a better future.

A Dead End?

*U*pon finishing this book, I read an article in which the author compared students' results on the SAT, an exam that approximately 48% of college-bound high school students take at the beginning of their senior year. The scores were compared taking into consideration race (white, black, and Hispanics; students of Asian background had similar results to the white students) as well as family income and the level of parental education. In these last two instances all races were jointly compared.

The statistics show that in 2003 out of a possible 1600 (800 in Verbal, 800 in Math) scores, on average, are at their highest, but not for us minorities; for us the results are at their worst. 36% of the students that take the SAT are members of a minority group.

An encouraging fact, though, is that 38% out of the students who take the SAT are the first member of their family to attend college, which means that, despite overwhelming odds, those students show clear aspirations for progress.

The average score for white students in 2003 was 1063 compared to 905 for Hispanics and 857 for blacks.

Ten years ago, Hispanic students were 127 points behind white students, whereas today they are 158 points behind. In ten years we regressed 31 points. Nevertheless, there exist some, however few, indications of positive trends in the Latin community. For instance, in the last ten years the number of Hispanic students taking the SAT with the intention of getting a college education increased by 50%.

Ten years ago black students were 187 points behind white students; today they are 206 points behind, a backward movement of 19 points.

Race is not the only factor that affects SAT results. They are equally affected by the regional gap between rural and urban schools (rural students are 68 points behind), as well as the disparity in the level of parental education (children of parents with a college degree are 272 points ahead).

Figures also show that there is a direct correlation between family income and SAT results: the higher the incomes, the higher the chances of children receiving a better education and thus getting far superior scores. Moreover, recent studies show that the new version of the SAT will deepen this gap. In this manner, the opportunities for our children are increasingly reduced.

We appear to be at a dead end, inside an infernal circle that prevents us from escaping. When you have a low income, you have fewer possibilities of sending your children to good schools. Consequently, your children and their children will have fewer chances to succeed in life.

This disparity is illustrated by the gap in SAT scores, with privileged kids receiving superior scores. Thus it becomes more and more difficult for our children to be accepted into a good college.

Yet this contemptible circle can be broken. By no means is it easy, but it can be broken. There is a path to success, I know it, we have found it, and our children have traveled it.

The Gold Rush

𝒰pon our arrival to the South of the United States, a friend told us, "this is the land of opportunities," a common phrase that was told to us untiringly in our native country.

For many years we have looked for such opportunities without ever reaching them, and still we are convinced that they exist. We know that you can only reach them through hard and relentless work, and so we have worked night and day in search of them, daydreaming about them, then falling asleep to look for them in our dreams.

We have searched for clues in the triumph of others, as well as in the failure of others. As if searching for the Holy Grail, we have looked for the way with the faith of the pilgrim that travels across the desert in search of the hidden garden.

Nonetheless, in spite of the many times people assure us that our ideas will bring us success, we have yet to reach such an opportunity. There has always been something stopping us; either an unexpected obstacle that blocks the road, or a wrong turn, or someone who locks the door just before we get in.

In our long sleepless nights, my wife and I, sad, with our stomachs half empty, converse, softly looking for ways to hide the cruel reality from our children. We strive to mask the distress in our eyes so as to allow them a certain happiness and instill in them faith in the future.

But, how can we explain to those who have already crossed the finish line what we feel when we run and run and never reach our goals? How can we describe to the fortunate, who have never run in search of opportunities for success, our exhaustion of both body and soul, our tired eyes, our weary dreams, our fear of dreaming a new failure, of closing our eyes and dreaming a new disillusion.

Years after our arrival to the United States, we read in a Spanish newspaper a column that featured successful Latinos. We never read a single column about those who struggle and fail, but continue fighting. They are the majority, but no one writes about them. I, on the other hand, believe we must write about these forgotten hopefuls because all successess are made out of dreams and failures, and often what seems like a failure can hold the seeds of triumph if one is capable of learning from his or her failures.

Maybe the problem is that we do not know how to dream, or what to dream so that our aspirations become realities. Maybe our dreams are so ambitious that we become blind to real opportunities.

Sleepless nights had shown us that bad dreams do not stay locked in our bedroom, but, rather, tiptoe into our children's beds, bringing with them fear and sadness. One night, feeling defeated, tossing and turning in our rackety bed, my wife and I were talking about the possibility of retracing our steps and going back home when we heard our daughter screaming with anguish "*Mami*, daddy!"

We ran to her bedside, hugged her and told her, "Don't be scared, it was just a bad dream, we are here beside you."

Back in our bed we looked at each other and asked, "What did she scream? *Mami*, daddy?" At that moment we realized that no return was possible. Our goals were clear now. Our opportunity in the land of opportunities was not as much for us as for our children. We realized that our main goal, the reason for our pursuit in this country was the future of our children.

Walking as silently as we could, we returned to our daughter's bedside and softly told her, "Don't worry, we are here for both you and your brother, and our task is to clear the way for you in this land of opportunities."

This path is by no means easy to follow; it is not easy to put your dreams aside, and I bear our life as a witness, but when you help your kids to reach their goals, the rewards are immense, and I bear our children as witnessess.

The Departure

When you leave your homeland, you leave it in search of a better life. You pack your illusions, the easiest things to pack, and you distribute your weary dreams, sometimes leaving behind a part of yourself waiting, promising yourself that you will return once you have made your dreams come true.

When I left, I left not in search of a better life, but simply to preserve my life.

Thinking it over, being able to preserve your life is in itself a better life, so when I look back I cannot be discontent.

City Lights

We arrived at Atlanta International Airport on a rainy evening. We sat the children in one of the four carts that we were going to use to move our luggage, and we waited for the bright metallic mouth to open and, tossing its long black tongue, set our seven cardboard boxes free; seven boxes that contained our belongings: toys, our children's Sunday clothes, pictures that captured forever a smile and the past, and a few books to teach our children our language.

First, the luggage pick-up set free the suitcases, beautiful suitcases that, full of pride and confidence, returned to the place where they belonged. They were followed by timid suitcases tied closed with a piece of rope that looked at the new environment with a mix of curiosity and shyness, trying to pass unnoticed. Behind them came all our cardboard boxes, tied up ten times around, for fear that someone would dare to open them and steal part of our dreams, boxes that would accompany us in our ventures and misadventures in this new land. The sight of our boxes provoked the festive screams of our two little children who in dancing choir counted *una, dos, tres* . . . as the boxes were passing through the luggage pick-up's gaping jaw.

We placed the boxes in our carts and then took a bus that took us to the parking lot of the airport where a van was waiting to pick up our family and our possessions. We toured Atlanta twice, our faces against the cold windows, our eyes dazzled by the lights. Beautiful lights that, shining far beyond the city limits, illuminated the clouds that embraced our arrival. After the second tour, our hearts pounding frantically, we got lost in the darkness of the countryside of the South of the United States, smuggling with us our dreams.

Lost In Space

We arrived at a small town lost in the rural stretches between Georgia and Alabama, detached from any intimation of urbanity or even time. Its main street crossed it from East to West, before vanishing behind the last group of houses.

From this main street hung some small side streets that in turn divided into alleys leading to the tiny neighborhoods whose invisible limits were only known by the city official in charge of dividing them into districts. The division was made to distribute the children among different schools, which close to downtown, beside the railroad tracks, near the chicken slaughterhouse and its sticky smell of fresh blood, and at the end of the abandoned houses of the black neighborhood, provided the kids with the education that would eventually allow them to make a living.

There were apparently three or four school districts dividing the downtown area, in addition to the "country school," which regrouped all the kids living in the rural area of the town.

As the years passed we found that the difference between good and bad schools is measured by the students scores on the state and national tests, as well as by its percentage of student retention. We also realized that this difference has a direct correlation with the racial and social composition of the population of each district.

The good schools are usually located in predominantly white districts, and the bad schools in districts with a population comprised primarily of minorities, whose income borders the poverty line.

Upon our arrival we rented a small, cheap two-bedroom house, which by chance was located between two different school districts, a good one, the downtown district, and a bad one, the district near the railroad crossing. To tell you the truth, the house was mistakenly included as a part of the downtown district, the one with the best school in town, as many believed. The town official in charge of classifying the houses mistook the back door, which faced downtown, as its entrance, which overlooked the railroad.

The opening of an immense new "city school" that would combine all those small districts, as the country school had done, was scheduled for the end of the year after our arrival. It was expected that this new school would end the division between good and bad schools so that all the children attending public schools would receive exactly the same education regardless of their race, or of their parents' economic background. This model school was developed thanks to funds from the newly created state lottery.

Out of our two kids only the girl was of the age for attending school. The day we went to enroll her in school the principal was not there. Her secretary asked us to sit on a wooden bench. Looking at us out of the corner of her eye she continued her lively phone chat with a man we presumed was her boyfriend from the laughs, sighs, and a few words that we picked up here and there.

Giving our papers a casual glance she interrupted her conversation for a second to ask us if our daughter spoke English and what grade was she in, in our country. Upon hearing our answer, on a marginal note she wrote, "Must repeat the grade."

At one point, tired of waiting we started to feel uncomfortable, but didn't dare to move or tell her we would be back some other day. We feared that if she got upset she would register our daughter a grade or two behind. Our new friends in town had told us this was the rule in this country.

We were pondering our predicament of whether or not to leave, when the door was opened and a middle-aged man, with a chubby face and bright smile entered the office. He greeted the secretary, and asked her what we were doing there, smiling at the children.

We explained to him that we had just moved into town and that we wanted to enroll our daughter in school. We told him that she didn't speak English yet, but that in our country she had proved to be an excellent student, and was capable of taking the second grade, where she belonged.

The kind man looked our daughter in her eyes, who in turned smiled at him from ear to ear, and glanced at her school records. Then, in a rudimentary Spanish, he asked us the name of the courses she had taken, and finally said, "She has exceptional grades. I am going to help you. I am a good friend of the principal's."

In fact, when the principal arrived, he went to her office taking our papers with him. Later on he called us to let us know that our daughter had been registered into the second grade, but that after a few months the principal would look at her progress and based on that she would decide whether or not to keep her in that grade.

A week later we asked for a day off from work to accompany our daughter to school. We drove her to the main entrance, kissed her goodbye, and watched as she, so small and frail, was engulfed by the sea of children.

Our fellow townspeople were angry that our daughter was attending this school. The residents of the downtown district got upset as well because she was attending a school where according to them we didn't belong, referring not only to our family, but also to all of us, the Hispanic people living in town, as if we had a place in the community from which, collectively, we should not stray.

Some time later the principal of the school called us to her office and told us that for the first three months of class our daughter didn't say a word. They had assigned her a special tutor to teach her English for two hours a day, but even she had not been able to make our daughter talk. Regardless, they had decided to keep her in second grade based on her grades on homework and tests, which showed she understood all that was taught in the classroom.

Back home we asked our daughter why she refuse to speak; if it was because the other children were making fun of her, or if someone had been cruel to her, or if it was simply that she didn't understand. Finally, tired of our questioning, she told us that she understood everything perfectly, that she was able to do her homework and to complete the tests, but that she didn't want to talk for fear of sounding different; she didn't want to offend the language. So, she had firmly decided to start talking only when she was sure of doing it right.

In fact, three weeks later she started to speak English with a beautiful Southern accent without ever suspecting that, years later, in another school in New Jersey she would once more remain silent, while losing her Southern accent so that no one could laugh at her differences.

She, the first one to go to school in this country, had taught us our first lesson: one needs to understand others and make oneself equally understood in order to be respected.

From then on we decided to speak only Spanish at home so our children could understand and be understood by their own, but in school, on the street, they would speak English. It was clear to us that we could permit ourselves to speak broken English, but that our children had to master it if they wanted someday to belong somewhere.

Years later we would understand how important it is for our children to feel confident, and not to feel out of place. We understood that feeling unsure of ourselves, as if we do not belong, eradicates all possibilities of success no matter how wonderful the opportunity in our hands appears to be.

Our first town taught us that there are different paths in life. For every situation, there are principal roads that lead you to a goal (and they are not the easier to travel) as well as dead end roads. Our first town taught us that for every situation we have to be absolutely clear about our goals, so we can choose the right path to follow. Our first town taught us that, once we had reached a goal, new challenges would come our way, and we would be compelled to choose again.

But, let's not get ahead of ourselves. Let's return to the beginnings.

The Wooden Blocks

Since the beginning of school we tried to support our daughter in any way we could, knowing by intuition that there would be a moment in which we would stay behind and she would have to go on without our help, with all our love, but without our practical help, and that situation made us panic.

Years later in New Jersey the mother of one of our son's classmates would brutally throw that reality into our face when, referring to our son, she told us, "In our school system, everything is basically easy until third grade, and all the kids can get good grades. From fourth grade on things change and classes are divided into different levels: advanced or honors, average, and remedial classes. From fourth grade on school becomes competitive and the help of the parents or paid tutors becomes very important in order for kids to cope with the work of the higher courses," she added.

Then, she asked us, "What is going to happen to your kids when you will not be able to help them? You will probably have to ask that they'll be placed in the regular courses where there's no competition."

Fortunately, our daughter, aware that she had all our support but that there were concrete limitations to our ability to help, discovered and understood how to learn from her own mistakes. She learned to switch languages, then to correct her accent, learning first the accent of rural Georgia only to change it later to the accent of New Jersey. She learned to enjoy foods of different flavors, while still reveling in the tastes of our country.

She used to study over and over every red mark that her teachers made in her English notebooks. If by any chance the mistake reappeared, she cried tears of frustration for having made it a second time.

After finishing her homework she usually fell asleep with her head on the kitchen table and we had to carry her to her bed. On the luckiest days, those in which she didn't have too much homework, we transformed their bedroom into a world of whims and fantasies.

From one of the old cardboard boxes we would remove our riches: enchanted books in which stories transformed the room into a castle, a ghost ship, or the blue bird of paradise that lead our steps to the country of dreams.

Our three years old son heard the stories and smiled, asking us to repeat them again and again. Even when half asleep he would correct us when we skipped a page.

Our son used to observe his sister working at the kitchen table, while he tried to imitate her by scribbling his "homework" on a paper. Without knowing it, he too was learning. Oftentimes we found him browsing through the old, heavy dictionary that never failed to answer his sister's question, "*mami, papi,* what does it mean?" Without yet knowing how to read, he determinedly turned the pages of the tattered book in search of the answers to a question he never posed.

On Sundays we used to go hunting for treasures. For a day, we walked the sidewalks of those houses we could only enter in our dreams to search through piles of objects the owners had discarded.

As expert treasure hunters we looked for puzzles, some in plastic or humble cardboard, others made out of wood. Puzzles that our children assembled with passion until being able to do it with their eyes closed. Once we found a set of wooden blocks with the letters of the alphabet inscribed on them. They came from the New York Museum of Modern Arts, blocks that a lucky traveler brought to the countryside of Georgia to teach his children, blocks that now were teaching our children.

Sometimes our daughter came carrying an old Barbie in her hands –a doll that had been rejected because it had lost the luster of its newness– to ask us if she could have it, our son carrying toy cars with two, three or sometimes four wheels. Back home they escaped in endless races all over their room, and the vroomm, vroomm prolonged the limits of their bedroom to boundless spaces.

Our son secretly began to learn by himself, as if illegally crossing the border between ignorance and knowledge. At a certain point, he asked to go to school with his big sister. We took it seriously, as we never laugh at our children's requests even if they ask for the moon. Too often we have been unable to grant them their wishes, but we have never laughed about them.

It was when our son asked us to enroll him in school that we realized how much he had learned in the course of emulating his sister. His scribbles had become letters that created magical words, his numbers now had a meaning, and the aged dictionary began to offer its secrets.

Grapes of Wrath

Throughout our first three years in this country we struggled desperately to improve our condition. We moved three times, every time renting a smaller house, and always telling the children, telling ourselves, that the next one will be our own house, but for the time being we need to save up.

My wife had a steady job, I had only sporadic jobs; for the most part I endlessly wasted my time filling out job applications. I applied to the chicken slaughterhouse and even though I promised the manager to accept without complaint the worst shifts or the tasks no one accepted, I was not hired.

They didn't hire me, even though I was recommended by a friend who, having arrived in this country a couple of years before, felt completely at home here, and had worked at the chicken slaughterhouse almost since his arrival.

Thus I was compelled to continue inventing useless jobs of my imagination, jobs that did not pay, but, rather, helped heal my soul with the illusion that I too was being productive and was creating my opportunities in the land of opportunities.

For over a period of a little more than a month I landed a job in Texas, after which I proudly returned home to fill the pot and buy our first and only luxury, a living room set; a gleaming living room set, later a worn collection of couches, that in years to come would perish in one of the many nights when, with our children, we sat to caress our dreams of a better life.

It was in our fourth year in the United States that we realized that it was not going to be us who would benefit from the better life that we sought when we left our country. We realized that we had to be ready to make all the sacrifices we could in order to open for our children the doors to that better life.

We realized that the opportunity for a better life in the land of opportunities was for our children and for their children, and that we had to be ready to sacrifice part of our own dreams so as to open their doors.

Integrated But Not Equal

One of the big differences that we noticed upon our arrival to the United States is the way children walk. The children from here, those who know they own something, walk straight, unfalteringly, overconfident. Our children, and the children of the underprivileged, walk slowly and shamefully, as if they didn't want to leave traces, as if avoiding being noticed for fear of the reaction of the other children. They walk as if reluctant to leave their footprint, ready, at any moment, to yield to others.

These children need to learn that you must walk leaving traces; that you must walk with your head up straight, without trampling others, but not allowing others to trample you. Life taught us that the first one to get to a crossroads is the one who gets to cross, and that you don't have to bend your back or let people step on you so they can advance in life.

We must teach our children that life is like a four-way intersection: If you always yield, you'll never get to cross. We must teach them that it is possible to be both amiable, and respectful and still cross; that they too have the right to go forward, and must go forward.

It is not easy to live in anger; hunger, frustration, and injustice generate anger and bitterness, but you cannot live in anger and bitterness without passing them on to your children. Bitterness stops you; anger prevents you from seeing a way out and at the end you collapse unable to see the horizon and thinking that everyone is against you. Yes, with anger we learned that resentment is a bad advisor.

It was difficult to make our children understand that they too have a future, as the other children in this country, and that it is up to them to set their limits. It was difficult to make them understand that our sacrifices were similar to the ones endured by the parents or grandparents of their new classmates (the sacrifices of the newly arrived) to open for them a path in life. It was difficult to make them understand that these hardships were normal, and that nothing was free in the land of opportunities.

Life taught us that in order to help our children we had to learn how to put our own dreams aside; we had to renounce special treats, a new pair of shoes, buying something beautiful just for the pleasure of having it, in order to save the money to buy what would improve our children's education. But most of all, life taught us that it is necessary to walk steadily, that you need to feel that you belong without asking permission from others. You may have a good job, or be attending the best school in town, but if you don't feel well, your efforts accomplish little, you learn just the minimum, or you quit the good college that eventually would help you land a good and well-remunerated job.

To Live In Debt

*I*n order to help our daughter walk steadily and leave traces in this, her new country, we decided to accept a first credit card, the first one that with the years came to be one of several.

Was it an error? No, I would rather say a horror because we didn't have options, but not an error because it was thanks to that damned credit that we were able to pay for dance classes for our daughter. We know that dance lessons are not essential, unless you want to give your children the opportunity to walk straight, their head high with the conviction that they too have the right to dream.

How can you explain to those who have everything that our children, who steal time from their rest in order to study more and be successful in school, have also the right to enjoy music, dance, art, and to move through life with an agile but steady step, and not timidly as if feeling ashamed?

We never used the credit to buy the superfluous. Our children know that at home we don't have a right to what is superfluous no matter how necessary that superfluous can seem so we can feel good when saying, "I bought this because it's pretty, because it tastes good, and not just because I need it." And sometimes we have to call a meal superfluous.

We never had the right to what is superfluous, but for whatever is vital to nourish the soul we always found the means thanks to new credit cards that, as a curse, pawned our future while constructing the future of our kids. For the "unnecessary" that was vital to grow intellectually and emotionally we always found the means; for that book that one would be able to read taking notes in its margins so as to speak at distance with the author, or that one we would highlight to interpret one's dreams; or for the gas to go from our distant small town to attend a free concert in a park in Georgia, and later in Central Park in New York, for that kind of "superfluous" things we always found the means.

I do not recommend that anyone get a credit card, unless it is vital to construct the future of your children. I warn you that whoever enters that fatal circle never comes out.

The Road

Once we decided to change the direction of our dreams, our goals seemed strangely clearer. They didn't seem easier, just clearer. It is possible to reach your goals without having a lot of money; it is painful, you cry and get so tired that sometimes even to breathe hurts, but it is possible, without having money, to find your way in the land of opportunities.

We had to give our children the possibility to talk with other kids without language barriers. We wanted to help them remember their own language, but at the same time make sure that they learned the new language well, the one that was foreign to us, language that would allow them to communicate with the people that from now on would also be their people.

We started to read to them in our language and make them read in English. A dictionary in hand, we urged them to learn words that they would probably not use in the daily life but that would help them understand better what they were reading and go beyond the first meaning, the one that in the future would limit their writing, their readings, and their chances in life.

We subscribed to a newspaper so they could know what was going on in the world and understand that they were part of that world.

We told to ourselves that it was not enough to teach them how to walk, we needed to teach them to walk alert on the path of life. We taught them that the path of life is not easy, that we fall down, that we get tired, that the price is high, but we also taught them that you learn fast and that step by step you can reach the finish line, and when you look back you can breathe, smile, look to the future and set yourself a new goal.

We must instill in our children the desire to be the best; for our children it is not enough to be just "good;" sometimes they see their chances denied because of that. People who do not accept that our society is changing want our children to stay in "their place" as lawn mowers, waitresses at parties, cooks, cleaning ladies, in short, the lowest jobs. Nonetheless, I strongly believe that our children have all that is needed to get wherever they want, and this is not arrogance.

It is not selfish ambition, but a scream that comes right from the heart. We all have the right to a peaceful sleep without fearing that the landlord will ask us to leave. We all have the right to send our kids on vacation. Yes, we have all the right to see that our children's rights are respected, to see that they are considered part of the "we" of the Declaration of Independence, and I have no doubts that one day a member of an ethnic minority will be President of this country.

The 3:10 Train Does Not Stop At Yuma

*F*leeing from the economic crisis that was striking the country, crisis that struck the rural Southern states with more strength, we decided to take the train and migrate up North, to more industrialized and populated areas, to New Jersey.

Jobs were getting scarce; lines at the unemployment office that was located outside the city limits were endless. The amount of free school lunches increased as the quality of the lunches decreased.

We said goodbye to the principal of the school, cleaned up our small house beside the railroad, watered our plants for the last time, and took a car that drove us to the next town to take the train. The train did not stop in our town.

Starting All Over Again

When we first arrived to New Jersey from Georgia, we had spent all our savings on the trip. Exhausted but happy we were looking forward to starting a new life. As a premonition, this time we arrived during the day.

Without being aware of it we had rented a small miraculously inexpensive house (the owner was leaving for Spain and needed someone to look after her property). The house was located in a town whose school system had a reputation as one of the best in the area.

We noticed that things were different in this town when the lady that was waiting for us with the keys, upon seeing us unloading our cardboard boxes mockingly asked when the moving truck would arrive. "In this town, when people move they hire a company that packs, load, transports, and unloads in the new house," she added. She gave us the keys, asked for the rent, and left. Meanwhile we continued unpacking our old boxes and spreading our wounded hopes in the living room of the new house while the kids played and happily counted *una, dos, tres*...

Fortunately, thanks to geographical distribution, our town's school system was joined with the school system of a neighboring wealthy town. They invested without hesitation in all that could represent improvement to their children's education, their children's and as contraband our children's too. But we were not aware of all that when we happily settled down in our new town in the land of opportunities.

Silent Films

𝑊e had just finished opening our boxes when someone knocked at the door. For a second we all smiled happily remembering the movies that we had seen in which nice neighbors accompanied by their children came to welcome you with a warm apple pie, and that while the parents conversed with each other the children became friends and would play in the street.

My wife got very nervous, but keeping calm she ordered immediately, "Take out the tea pot, and boil the water to offer them a cup of tea. And you,' she ordered me, 'unpack the cups."

No, it was not the friendly neighbors who were knocking at the door to welcome us into town. It was the cable TV man, who was offering to reconnect the cable. We asked for prices (exorbitant for our resources) and we kindly sent him away telling him that we had just moved into town and that we preferred to take some walks in the woods and go to the beach, that we wanted to get to know the area before school started and therefore we would not have the time to watch TV. "We will call you later on," we added. Up to date he is still waiting for our call.

In fact, that's what we did, we went on walks and strolls with our children, and conversed with them. After four o'clock when the entrance was free, we used to go to the beach, build sand castles, and shivering, hand in hand to gather up our courage, we dared to go in the water defying the iced waves.

We found out that the public library lent videos of old movies for free, and in the evenings we sat down watching movies of Charlie Chaplin, Houston, John Ford, Woody Allen, Stanley Kubrick and so many others.

Thanks to the lack of money, without noticing it, our children got a world class cinematographic culture that helped them later on to write school essays, analyze other movies, read the books in images, and have a broader vision of the world, our small world.

The lack of TV gave my wife and I more time for love, our children more time to study, and gave all of us more time to talk and play together.

That extra time after school gave our children the possibility of leveling up, and then, of reaching the highest levels in their respective grades. Even though apparently the curriculum was the same in the North and in the South, there was a huge difference with the rural schools of Georgia.

The weekends, never during the week, we

sat back in front of our old second hand TV bought in a lost town in the countryside of Georgia for the most awaited moment for all of us, *la película familiar*, the family movie.

We laughed together with the genius of Charlie Chaplin or Woody Allen; we cried together with *Casablanca*. In family agreement we used to stop the movie to fix something to eat most of the time toasts with margarine, the best times a pack of chips or cheetos that left our fingers all orange but appeased our hunger for eating the same food as everybody else.

Five years later, at a soccer tournament of our son's team, during a long break between games we went to a big mall that sheltered many movie theaters. After a careful examination of our budget we decided to treat ourselves to a new released movie for the first time in the United States. We chose *Notting Hill* with Julia Roberts.

On leaving the theater we were walking with steadier steps, and full of happiness, we returned to the soccer field. We felt almost like normal people. We had watched a movie when it was in its first weeks, we didn't have to wait years until the library decided to buy it, and our kids got to school talking about it when no one remembered it.

Nevertheless, we didn't see that as a tragedy, on the contrary, from time to time the kids were able to discuss with some of their teachers a classical movie; or our daughter once in high school was able to write an essay on the evolution of Dustin Hoffman's performing career from *Mid-*

night Cowboys to *Rainman* to *Wag the Dog*. And strangely, we were able to look without sadness, and perfectly understand the dreams of the deprived, the tragicomical situations caused by the lack of money. As they, we got indignant with injustice, and as they, we also dreamt of a better life.

Gone With the Wind

When school started, the people in our neighborhood got used to seeing us hand in hand with our kids walking to school, and kissing them goodbye.

We arrived very proud to the first parents and teachers conference and we waited for our turn to see the teachers. First we had to talk with our daughter's teachers. With a smile, used to the fact that our kids had always had the best grades in school we asked just as a formality, "How is she doing?" Luckily we were sitting. Two of the teachers in two different rooms told us practically using the same words that in school they had special classes for children like ours, that if we agreed they could placed them in those classes; that we needed to think about it, but that of course it had to be our decision, not theirs.

Once in the hall in complete distress we leaned against the wall trying to understand what they meant. When the Social Studies class teacher saw us, asked us to go to her room and told us: "I see that you have already talked with the Math and English teachers. They came to see me and asked me to give the children a test to measure their intelligence. I spoke with the children and they are adorable and smart; not very well prepared academically though, but brilliant, and I have no doubt they will level up very quickly. You have every right to say no,' and lowering her voice she added, 'the school must accept your decision and can't do anything against it."

Almost running, we returned to the other teachers' rooms and when seeing us so determined and defiant the two teachers said as if to stop us from speaking: "OK, this is your decision, the results will tell who is right."

Yes, we made our choices. We chose that our kids level up and excel; we chose the way of academic excellence knowing that this path would open for them the doors to a better future. We didn't choose the easy path because we know what our kids are capable of, and today we also know our rights, and we would have never allowed them to be placed in the special classes where the children are practically taught nothing. Other kids were not as lucky as ours; the school sent them back a grade or two. "They don't speak the language," schools usually say, but that is the easy way for the schools, and definitely not the best way for the kids.

It is true that we spoke, and still speak broken English, but our children spoke English well, with a Southern accent, but good English, and they spoke it better every day. Six months later they both were at the top in all their classes, not because they wanted to compete against the other students, but because they wanted to be there, had worked for it and deserved to be there; because we had already figured out that the only way to succeed was to triumph in academics, and that, for a foreign kid being good is not enough.

No, we didn't allow anyone to limit our children's possibilities because of the color of their skin, because of the poor preparation they got in the first school they attended, because of their accent, or their second hand clothes.

In the evenings we organized competitions to practice the times-tables, and usually the kids were the winners; usually, not always because they had to understand that they were in a race and that it was not easy to win. They had to understand that no one but themselves would clear them the way.

When they had to decide on a foreign language to study they chose French, they knew Spanish already, and it would have been too easy to choose Spanish. They learned to ask questions, and if they were not satisfied with the answers to do their own research until being satisfied.

The road for a better life is hard and painful, but you can win the battle, my children. And so, the day will come in which you will not be hungry. No one will ever see in your faces that wince of pain that rejection can cause. And I lift my fist to heaven with God as my witness, as Scarlet, heroine of *Gone With the Wind* exclaimed when she arrived to her destroyed fields to start all over.

Explanations

*H*ow difficult it is to explain to he who does not know hunger what it means to spend three days without eating waiting for the next salary to arrive.

How difficult it is to explain this when in the room next door our daughter was practicing and practicing for the SAT (the test that kids must take in order to apply for college) because she had already decided that she wanted to go to the best college possible in the United States and for that and to get the necessary scholarships she knew she needed excellent results.

It is true that sometimes we didn't have enough food to put on our table, or our meals were somewhat frugal, but it is also true that money was never scarce for a book to practice for the SAT. True, the SAT books prepared our daughter to enter to the college of her choice, but hunger and deprivations prepared her for life.

How difficult it is to explain how much pain there is behind every success of our children, and how easy it is to explain how that pain transforms into happiness when they get results that answer to their expectations, results that help them get closer to their goals.

Honors behind Doors

A stage in our children's life was staying behind. The day our daughter graduated from junior high, her Math teacher (the same one that once wanted to send her to the special courses) stopped us in the school parking lot and gave her an award in secret, asking her not to tell anyone. The award she got in the French class was delivered to her not in the public ceremony, but in the classroom, and so on. But all that didn't really matter anymore; because of her grades she was recommended to take honor classes in high school.

Our son attended junior high for three more years. With our daughter in high school, for those three years he had to endure alone all kinds of racist jokes against Latinos. When he told us the stories he used to comfort himself saying, "It is not serious, they are just kids making jokes, they don't want to hurt me on purpose."

In the town next to ours, one night the neighbors found racist flyers protesting against the presence of blacks, Latinos and Jews in town, for the alleged preference that the public school system shows on their behalf thus denying opportunities to the pure white population. "What is it left for our kids?" they complained. The parents were protesting because the school had suspended three students who during lunch hour had insulted another kid: "We don't like niggers here!" In the other town, the one with which we share the high school, neighbors found swastikas drawn in front of the junior high.

It doesn't happen every day, it is not all the kids or all the parents who do that, but it happens, and it is dangerous.

Our son was beaten in the lockers, not every day, not by all the kids, but it happened a few times, and when it happened he was either late for class or to get back home. One afternoon when he was coming back home he had an accident. He was running away from a bunch of kids, but didn't ride his bike fast enough and the kids put a stick in his front wheel. The speed plus the weight of the backpack in which he carried all his books and notebooks since the day he found his locker opened and his books and notebooks semi-destroyed made the front wheel of the bike skid and, he fell down, his headfirst. Luckily we had bought him a helmet.

The next week, there was another incident. Playing soccer during lunch in the schoolyard a kid lifted him, and threw him on the floor headfirst. He passed out for a couple of minutes.

That same afternoon we went to see the school principal. When his secretary saw us she told us that the principal was waiting for us, and asked us to wait a few seconds. We asked ourselves why was the principal expecting us, we went to see him for a totally different thing, to make sure that our son was really in the advanced courses because he was not with the same kids of the previous years.

When we got to his office he listened to us and assured us that our son was in the advanced classes. As a matter of secondary importance he mentioned that there had been a small accident during lunchtime involving our son and another kid, but nothing serious. He had already talked with the other kid and his parents. He finished the interview with us by adding that, "your son too has his character, you know".

Once at home our son didn't want to tell us what had happened, so we went to one of his classmates to ask him, and so we found out. Terrified, we told his classmate's father about the incident with the bike, and we told him that from that moment on we would pick our son up from school. When we were leaving, his classmate's father told us that the days we would not be able to pick him up he could walk home with his son and wait for us there. "My son is older,' he added, 'they will not dare to tease him."

Sometime later, when the pain was unbearable, our son put in writing what had happened, his feelings about it, and what he had not told us. It was his way of surviving, his way of protecting his heart from exploding. As title, he wrote Yo, and then his name, and it was published, in English, as *Yo, Alejandro, my/our Story*. Though the book didn't bring him complete acceptance, at least it earned him respect and personal security. He had won his first battle, to exist, and his right to live in peace.

He graduated valedictorian from junior high, and as is the tradition, his name was engraved on a plaque in a wall of the school. Yes, a stage was left behind.

It is true, it doesn't happen every day, but it happens, and that is serious. The sorrow our children felt because of it, we felt it too, and the tears that they didn't shed, we shed them in their name.

The Challenge

We all knew that high school represented the greatest and most serious challenge of all. Every class taken, every grade received would, in one way or another, determine the future. Six years had gone by since our children took their first steps in school taking with them the last vestiges of childhood.

Looking back at those years on the first day of high school we reminisced of the wooden blocks bought in the Southern countryside of the United States, or the cardboard letters that helped our daughter to learn how to read in our country, and we suddenly realized how useful they had been.

Before even thinking of sending them to school they had started to learn in their games. They not only learned the letters, but the intrinsic foundations of language structure so when they went to a real school they already knew how to read easy texts, write simple words and phrases, and read and write their names. Language allowed them to exist.

Playing, they also learned the numbers, not in order, in disorder, as disorganized as the letters in the beginning, but learning the numbers this way taught them to think mathematically which would help them later on to develop a logical reasoning structure.

Probably, that early start helped them to structure their mind in such a way that they can comprehend the world without getting lost in distracting details. It gave them the structure to understand the secrets of addition, the stinginess of subtraction, the wonders of division, the miracle of bread and fishes in infinite multiplication.

The puzzles, the letters that erected mysterious fortresses, the numbers that gave shape and soul to the old cardboard boxes *una, dos, tres*, were constructing the road to their future, were providing the clues that step by step were assembling the whole.

Life taught us that we not only need to have a very early start, but that we need to set out for life without any limitations, and most importantly with a strong belief in our children and their future. Otherwise, we will cut their wings.

Getting Ready for the Big SATep

To our good fortune, the last two years of junior high New Jersey schools participate in a program for talented youth sponsored by Johns Hopkins University, and the kids who qualify are able to take the SAT I. The same SAT taken by the college bound students, they take full of pride.

We were lucky our children qualified to take it. To qualify kids need a very high grade in Math or in English. Not many kids from our school were able to take it, not too many had qualified. Nevertheless . . .

Nevertheless, later on we learned that you do not need to qualify to take the test. Any thirteen year old kid from any state, not only from the states in which Johns Hopkins sponsors their programs, can register with the College Board to take the SAT when they are in seventh or eighth grades. The only difference is that the scores are not sent to the Johns Hopkins Programs for state awards or certificates of recognition, but any kid can take it as a diagnostic test to know where he is at, and what he still needs to do; as a practice to feel more confident when the moment of taking the SAT for real arrives.

Unfortunately, many kids do not take it thinking that if they didn't qualify they are not smart enough to take advantage of this opportunity. Others simply live in states that are not part of the group in which Johns Hopkins sponsors its programs and do not have knowledge of this option. Nobody cares to let them or their parents know about it, and when we do not have the money to invest in expensive tutoring to correct the lack of preparation we need to know about all these free opportunities. We need to put chances on our side.

The registration for the test has the same price as the registration for the normal SAT, around forty dollars, but how could you deny your kid something they have won with their own work and merits! We registered our children, and we were sent a brochure to help them get acquainted with the test. Their teachers told us that the kids didn't need great preparation, that they were not expected to score very high, and that anyway their scores would not be reported to any college, so they didn't matter.

Life has taught us that when someone says, "That doesn't matter" it's because it matters twice as much. We read the brochure we received from a different perspective, not the perspective of what was not expected from the kids, but rather what was actually expected from them, why did the program exist, why was it considered a distinction, and what it was good for.

We went to a big bookstore in our neighboring town, and for free, we browsed all the books they had to prepare for the SAT, and also the books that talked about colleges and universities in the United States. The second kind of book taught us that there were ranking lists for the universities, and the highest ones in the ranking required higher results on the SAT and in school grades. They also taught us that the raw scores up to 1600 had a direct correlation with the ranking of colleges: the higher you scored, higher your possibilities were of being accepted into the top colleges; and we guessed, the better the colleges, the better the opportunities.

We found out that the questions both on the English and Math portions of the test had three levels of difficulty. Out of all the questions, the junior high children were expected to answer correctly the easiest ones plus a few of average difficulty.

All the books to prepare for the SAT (and we studied all of them before investing our scarce resources) insisted upon the importance of how to approach the test. Not satisfied with the few exercises of the brochure that we had received, we bought a first book to prepare for the test. The race for college had begun; the children had still to complete high school, but the race for college had already started.

At home, our daughter, the first one to embark on that race, told us: "There are questions on the Math portion that deal with Geometry and Algebra, and I have not taken any of those classes yet. What shall I do?"

We started asking here and there, and so we found two programs from Princeton, one for Algebra and Geometry, and the other one for English, vocabulary, and text analysis. Just what the kids needed to face the test without so much stress, without the fear of not having yet covered all the subjects included.

That night, we looked at the calendar, we counted the days we still had left, and we prepared a plan. Our daughter started studying the books while her mother prepared flashcards with the list of words that the books mentioned were the most common on the SAT. On one side she wrote the word, on the other the definition and some clues that could help to memorize it. We took some time to study them, and that night we had the very first competition, to encourage our children's learning. I was disqualified twice by both our daughter and our son who, once more, had quietly started getting ready on his own.

Because at home we do not give up easily, I avenged myself by learning more and more lists of words until the day before the SAT, holding competitions with my daughter every time she was free.

We are lucky we do not give up easily, and aren't ashamed of asking for a second chance because after grading the first practice test our daughter looked at us alarmed and started immediately to check her answers and find out where and why she had failed.

Since they were little, our kids learned to get ready for competition, because life is a competition. They knew that the secret to getting better results was to have a head start, moreso when you do not have the means to pay private tutors that cost a fortune, at least for us. They knew too well that the secret is in practice, that if there is something they do not understand they can always ask their teachers for free.

One Saturday morning we took our daughter to take the SAT, the college bound students' test, and take it with them, in the same rooms. Not too many kids were taking it; not all the ones who qualified registered, and not all the kids in school had qualified.

We waved our daughter goodbye and saw her disappear within a group of high school students that looked at her with tenderness seeing her so small. She arrived at the classroom door, turned her face to say goodbye, and self-confident she entered the room, taking a first steadfast step on her way to college, on her way to the future.

Years later, when our son qualified to take it, we found out that there was another test called PLUS given to fifth and sixth graders for which kids did have to qualify. As with the SAT, we thought that only the children living in the states in which Johns Hopkins has its programs for talented youth could participate because in Georgia, where we used to live before, our daughter had not taken it.

We missed a practice test due to ignorance. Today we know that any kid in any state who qualifies can take the PLUS. The only difference is that, again, they are not considered for the certificates of recognition awarded by the Johns Hopkins Center for Talented Youth. Only the kids living in the states in which Johns Hopkins sponsors programs are considered. Our daughter could have taken it, we could have registered her, she had that right, but we didn't know it. That experience taught us to be more alert to the opportunities out there for our kids.

She Must Be Silly Miss Gloria

A few weeks went by before we got the results. When the envelope arrived we didn't open it, we went to pick her up at school and we gave it to her; it was her privilege to open it.

1010 out of 1600, which for a seventh grade kid was a very good score. Years later our son would score 1110; he started to get ready with his sister. Not satisfied with that score he took the test in eighth grade and score 1250. He was also paving his way to college.

They both qualified for the summer camps organized by Johns Hopkins, special programs with college teachers who help the kids go further and get better results in school. Unfortunately, those programs were very expensive, a fortune we could not afford, and neither of our children would benefit from them.

We both knew that there was a moment in which our financial reality worked against us.

That's why we needed to have a head start, to reduce the disadvantages and avoid staying behind in the middle of the race. Though it was true that we didn't have the money to pay for expensive camps or tutors, at least, taking the test implied having an extra practice, and the kids needed to take advantage of this opportunity.

Seven years later at a family reunion in Brooklyn the daughter of a cousin of our children who also lived in New Jersey was saying, dying laughing, that she had just taken the SAT in seventh grade and that had scored 600. "Silly Miss Gloria, my teacher,' she added, 'sent my parents a letter telling them that I needed to prepare better for the SAT, that I needed a tutor. That is so silly,' she continued 'a tutor, when I still have six more years to go before taking the SAT that counts."

No, you don't have six years. You need to learn to read the calendars. Remember, we need to have a head start, we do not have the right to wait until the last minute, it will be too late. Silly but caring; Miss Gloria just wants to give you all the possibilities to construct a successful future.

Her aunt, mother of four was carefully following the conversation, probably thinking of the future of her little kids. She asked our children if they had also taken the test in seventh grade, and what their results had been. When hearing their scores she asked them what had they done to prepare, and their answer was "practice," practicing every time we had a moment to spare.

She looked at her niece and told her: "You see? If they did it, you too can do it, you too can get 1100." We agreed with her that her little niece could also get a high score, we didn't agree with giving her a limit.

At home, we never set a top goal, we rather set bottom lines under which the results are not accepted because they just lead to failure and marginality. On the one hand, setting goals too high and unrealistically can lead to frustration, so those kinds of goals are dangerous. On the other hand, setting a top that is simply acceptable can limit our kids, making them content with less when they are capable of going farther.

The top goal must be infinite, and it is different for every kid. It is the one that makes them feel fulfilled and satisfied with their achievements, the one that allows them to step confidently on conquered grounds, the one that will open their doors and opportunities.

It is not easy to find a balance, on the one hand kids should not feel stressed, there is nothing worse than living with stress; on the other hand we don't have the right to limit their horizons.

The bottom line is that you have to set minimum goals, but you must always remind your kids that a result that closes doors, failing as a result of lack of work and effort is not acceptable.

At the top, there should be no limits. Encourage your children to push their limits up each time higher, but to always remember that reaching a goal must bring them happiness and content, and not frustration and sorrow.

Baby Steps, Giant Steps

We all knew that every step of school was important, but starting in high school they were twice important. Starting in high school the tracks would show, and most importantly would determine the future of our kids.

Having taken the SAT in seventh and eighth grade with meritorious results had given our children a strong feeling of self-confidence. It allowed them to realize that they were capable of fighting and winning; that no one could look down despicably on them, that they too must be taken into account.

Having taken the SAT in junior high prepared them better both academically and mentally to take the test in eleventh grade, the first SAT which results were reported to colleges.

Being realistic we knew that the results of the SAT in junior high were not even close to the bottom line of the results they would need three years later in high school when the moment to apply for colleges arrived, in case they wanted to get the necessary scholarships to attend a good school.

No, high school was not easy. The children were not permitted to rest on their laurels, and we were not allowed to rest either. Once more we were sleepless trying to figure out how could we help them.

TV shows got lost in time, but not the old movies we reserved for the weekends. The books to prepare for the tests got stockpiled; the exercises completed and erased to be used over and over.

More and more words were added to our competitions. We subscribed to *Time* magazine; besides knowing what was going on by reading the newspaper, the kids also needed to know it in the words of those who create opinion. They needed to acquire a language to complement the one they learned in the novels and poems studied in class and the limited language of the schoolyard conversations.

We had read what every college was looking for in the students, and we wanted them to want our children.

We knew high school was not going to be easy, as junior high had not being easy. This time the race was not against their schoolmates but against all the kids in the state and in the nation, against the kids of the ones that had arrived years ago to this country, and also against the newly arrived.

Experience taught us that, the same way the long road to the mastery of the language had started with some humble cardboard letters or wooden blocks, the road to college started with the results of the first tests taken in ninth grade. Year by year each and every grade counted to build up the grade point average that would distinguish him or her from the rest of the applicants applying to the same college and/or scholarship.

At the beginning of the first semester of high school the guidance counselors gave us a study plan for the four years; in bold we could see the dates of the state exams as well as the dates for the PSAT, and the SAT. They advised us to take the PSAT in junior year and the SAT in senior. Everything looked very well organized.

We have four whole years of high school ahead of us, we told ourselves; we still have time. Nonetheless a soft voice inside our head warned us: "You are making the wrong calculations. If you want to win you must have a head start, you must give yourselves time to correct any bad result on the way. Remember that your kids need more preparation time because they do not have tutors; their tutors are their own books and making books talk takes some time."

High School

The high school was bigger than the junior high. Every year it opened its doors to the children of two towns multiplying the experience by two. Once more two different groups were meeting, once more you had to make a choice, to stay within the children of your town, and among them with your own, or to open up, or at least try to open up to an ampler world.

Our children got to high school in a very advanced academic standing, and in the case of our son, he had also gained a large body. The kids that had thrown him to the ground or had put sticks in the front wheel of his bike were in low-level courses and their lockers were located far from his. High school didn't look easy, but it looked more amiable.

Other kinds of sticks appeared in the road. Our children had grown. They had acquired a better understanding of life, and looked at it with less innocent, but fortunately more alert eyes. The school was not too different from other schools except that it had a well-deserved excellent reputation for its academic programs, but within the different levels drugs wandered. They sneaked all over for self-consumption and for sale. Sometimes they came via older siblings already in college; dealers didn't need to take risks. One way or another drugs always found their way to the school and their effects were trivialized. Parents repeated: "It is proven that marijuana is less harmful than tobacco,' or 'since they are going to do it anyway (and that is inevitable), we prefer that they do it at home. It's a matter of protection for them so they will not get exposed to junk that can harm them."

Side by side with the drugs came alcohol, a proof of adulthood, freedom and independence. Some eight graders started to get ready for high school getting drunk over summer vacation. By doing that they expected to fit in high school. They also smoked their first cigarettes to graduate to adulthood.

With all kinds of drugs and alcohol roaming around it seemed that the healthiest thing left was just to risk cancer by smoking in the bathrooms or in the empty classrooms. In short nothing different from any other high school. Our position was not to criticize, we just warned our kids and taught them to say no to drugs and alcohol without feeling belittled; the pressure of the environment and the peer pressure were huge.

Drugs entered school as a means of gaining popularity and social promotion; drugs entered school as a means for being accepted and improving your self-esteem; drugs entered school as a business to make money and to imitate others by buying whatever the others had; and sometimes drugs (as well as alcohol) entered school as a continuation of homes, as a simple imitation of the example they had in their parents. As my father used to say, never raise your hand against a woman. If you hit your wife, your son will hit his, and the chain will perpetuate.

Fortunately, our children had acquired both the wisdom to consider "saying no" an option, and the strength to actually say no. They had also acquired the wisdom and the strength to stand out in other areas, in what they were strong, and not in what others wanted to push them to do. The fights they had to give on academic and ethical grounds had similar rules, and one supported the other.

They knew it was not going to be easy; that at the beginning they were going to be laughed at and the other kids would look at them as weird, but they also knew that after a while kids would stop their pressure and would look at them with respect, or would simply ignore them.

Nobody talks about that, the negative aspects of the school. It is an open secret, but you can't talk about it because that implies accepting that there is a problem, it implies that we have to face our children, that we have to look at ourselves in the mirror and face ourselves.

No more, no less than what happens in other schools. Our message to our children is clear: do not run that race; the one who wins it loses.

    We taught our children to avoid danger, and to avoid exposing themselves to danger, but we also taught them that if they were ever witnesses of an injustice, if someone ever tried to trample them or the weakest, they had to speak up against it. We taught them that there are some kinds of danger that you have to avoid, and others that you have to face if you don't want to feel dirty.

Objective vs. Subjective

Our children were aware that they had to take advantage of the tests graded objectively; when you add or subtract numbers there is no problem. They were also aware that when a degree of subjectivity came into consideration they lost, as if the sound of their names activated a trigger that lowered their grades.

The worst situations were found in English class. They had to put all their efforts into the vocabulary tests that were more or less objective, and do any extra credit offered. They knew that their grades would be lowered when the teachers corrected their essays. They would find them either "too creative" or "not creative enough," and the children would never get a clear explanation of what was wrong, they only got congratulations for the grades because "Those results are considered good in this school." It's true that their grades were considered good in the school, but we don't have the right to be just "good." When we enter the race we need more than a "good" to put all the chances on our side because in the competition our "goods" become average.

How to explain to the teachers that though the road is the same for everyone it presents different obstacles for everyone? How to explain to them how much we would have wanted that our children had more time to rest or play instead of getting up earlier to have a final review before a test in order to ensure success not only on the test but in life?

The Ones Left Behind

It was not a smooth road. Throughout the four years of high school the honor courses, the ones that would eventually open the doors to the best universities, started to decrease in size, as some students could not follow the rhythm. The fight was harder each year. All the kids knew that the spots in good universities were limited.

It was not easy to remain in those courses not counting on the same resources. In the case of our children, it would have been impossible for them to follow the rhythm of those courses without having had a head start. Yet the pressure to abandon is huge; from our own, those that had abandoned the race, had followed another path, a path of "easy money right now to live my life," meaning going to clubs, buying expensive clothes, a car, and any new gadget on the market. Their future and their children's future seem so far away and require so many sacrifices that it is better to give up on them.

Pressure comes also from certain classmates

who despise the ones who study, that label or isolate them and make them feel ashamed of being good students. You do not talk about studies; that's not cool. For these kids competition in that area is worthless.

How difficult it is to keep the children on track when they grow up and everything is studied to make them leave the race! The other students don't care; their future is within their reach, but our children must care, their future they have to invent.

Temptations are so powerful: making yourself accepted, being like them, being popular, believing to have succeeded when you reach the place they have reserved for you, at the bottom, and they make you feel accepted, provided that you remain in that place.

How can we teach our kids to find the balance between study and pleasure? How to explain to them that study must be a pleasure; that you must see it as the field of an Olympic game with its rules, difficulties but also the rewards of the most coveted sport?

How to explain to them that we too would like to go to a restaurant, to the movies, instead of using the money to buy the necessary books to prepare the SATs, as many books as we can give them, as many opportunities as we can within our scarce resources? It is not easy to live a life of sacrifices, oh, no! You get tired, and at moments of weakness you start to think that the others are probably right, and that you need to content yourself and abandon the race; you get to think that opportunities in the land of opportunities must be searched where we are allowed to, within the scraps.

How to find the balance in our life so our children can grow and develop proudly and happily in every aspect and we can live a happy life too? It is very hard to find it, there's no recipe, rules are created day by day and finding the balance is different for each family.

That's indeed part of the secret, a balance within the family. It is a shared responsibility, if the family's support is not behind it, no sacrifice will bear fruit. Schools must know it; the world must know it; our kids must know it. They are not fighting this battle alone.

The Calendar

*H*ighlighted in the calendar the high school gave us were the principal steps to follow in order to get to college, as well as the dates they recommended to take the required tests.

The dates and times for some of the tests are set in advance either by the State or nationally, and all the kids of the state or the nation take them at the same time. At the end of high school all the kids need to complete more or less the same amount of tests except for some subject tests called SAT II's. These ones are required only by some colleges depending on the degree you want to obtain; the high-ranking universities usually ask for three. The results of these tests are reported in the college applications, and admission officers take them into consideration in making their decisions.

State exams are needed to pass high school; the results do not count for college, but they are vital to graduate.

The calendar prepared by the school

showed that getting good results on the first try, with a bit of luck that is, kids had to take first the PSAT, then the SAT I and finally three SAT II if they wanted to apply to the best universities, five tests in four years. The PSAT was scheduled in eleventh grade (The PSAT is a shorter and easier version of the SAT; it serves as a diagnostic test, and to qualify for a national merit scholarship), and the other tests in twelfth grade.

You could read the calendar in two different ways: One exclaiming, "Oh! I still have time!" And the other one saying "Ugh! I don't have enough time, I need to hurry."

At a parents meeting, the guidance counselor told us that as a measure for improving the results on the PSAT, the school sponsored a practice test in tenth grade. This practice test would allow the kids to know where they were standing as well as suppress the fear of the test when they had to take it the following year. The money to pay for the test came from the school's PTA, so the test would be free of charge for the students but in junior year we had to pay for it.

We found this an excellent idea, to take a preparation test, and for free. Once at home we thought, if they get a head start because they want better results in all the kids of the school, and it is legal to do it, that means that they are doing what we have being doing with our kids, an early depart in order to get farther.

That night my wife and I went to sleep feeling proud of us. Without telling each other we both thought, we had already figured that out, and we are not from here.

The next morning when we were walking to our old car to go to work, we were both paralyzed in front of the same vision: we saw ourselves at the starting line of a car race. When we looked to our sides we saw brand new cars with powerful engines, and we could not get a better car, the engine of our old car purred happily but was not able to get beyond 50 miles per hour. Very far away we could see the finish line, and sitting there all the other drivers were waiting and laughing at us.

We returned home, took a look at the calendar once more and told ourselves: if the nationals or the ones that have lived in this country for years plan an early start to beat or at least tie with others like them, we have to plan a much earlier start to beat or at least tie them, to give ourselves a minimum chance of winning the race.

We told our daughter, you have to take the PSAT not just as a practice, as they told you, you must think this is the real PSAT and prepare yourself to win. Otherwise, it will not be worth it. So, in order to take real advantage of this extra practice, the summer before her tenth grade she completed another SAT book.

Yes, the calendar is read in different ways, it all depends on the car you are driving. The older it is, the earlier you have to depart. And in the race to college, in the race to the future having a head start is permitted and it is not considered cheating.

Strategies: Let's Eliminate

You must learn to eliminate, we told our kids. When we saw their gloomy faces we immediately added, "It sounds terrible, heartless, arrogant but if you want to win you must narrow down your choices of answers on the SAT. You eliminate one, and you have one possibility in four of getting it right; you eliminate two and have 33% chances; you eliminate three and have 50%. Yet if you don't have a clue it is better not to guess, the price is too high. The more you eliminate to make an educated guess the more opportunities you have to get a right answer; the more you try to guess without elimination, the more chances you have to get a wrong answer, which will lower your SAT scores. This is a unique time in which being ambitious is bad advice."

We not only had to elaborate our own calendar to succeed, we had to create our very own strategies too. Almost as a game we compiled and summarized the strategies proposed in every book, and based on them, the kids elaborated their own: study and memorization of "hot" words, as they are called, review of elemental Math concepts, practice and practice.

First they practiced without timing, and then they took a section of a practice test with timing, then two, then a whole test, three and a half hours. They had to learn to concentrate for three and a half hours, to control the time for every section, to make crucial decisions, to skip the questions which answer they didn't know to get back to them later.

And so by eliminating they impeded others from eliminating them, they got ahead, but that required preparation, and we needed additional time to prepare. We must have an earlier start so we can get farther; the earlier you plan your start the farther you will get.

You also have to count on the unexpected. As if by magic, the requirements are changed every year and nobody warns us about that. Every year there are more kids with better scores and the competition becomes more and more difficult.

Tests change as well, and the schools will need to adapt to them. The SAT dropped the section on analogies and added more paragraphs for reading comprehension. The perfect score will change from 1600 to 2400, and instead of only two sections it will have three segments: reading, writing and math.

To do well on the reading and writing segments it will not be enough to recognize the words, you must know how to use them in context, and understand the meaning of the paragraphs. The new reading section will feature at least one fictional passage on every test; this section intends to measure a student's ability to analyze something new.

The writing section will be divided between multiple-choice questions on grammar and style, and an essay on an assigned topic that the student must write in 25 minutes.

The Math portion includes concepts of Algebra II, while before it was only Math, basic Geometry and basic Algebra.

In essence, the test is changing from a test of general-reasoning abilities into a test of what kids learn in school, and because there are enormous differences in the quality of schooling in the country, kids who attend poor quality schools will be disadvantaged.

In the end nothing changes for us except that now our children need to prepare even more if they want to do well. They have to master the language, go further in the knowledge of Math, and study harder to get farther.

We know that for the hardest sections of the test, the people who have money will pay tutors for their kids as they have always done, so their offspring get the extra push they need. We can only buy a couple of books more to help our son get ready, and he has to start the race even earlier.

The calendar is still the same, for them and for us, minorities and non-wealthy people, but the timing still needs to be different if we want our kids to have a chance in the race.

Taking the SAT in seventh or eighth grade

was a first preparation for our children. It helped them to know where they were standing, and what they needed to correct. It helped them to learn to manage their time, and not to be stressed or scared.

The experience has taught us that in the land of opportunities we need to see life and education as a sport. You need to play happily otherwise it is not worth it and you cannot bear the effort. But you have to play to win otherwise the effort is worthless.

Getting ready for the game is not cheating, it is taking advantage of the opportunities; it is putting the chances on our side.

Undermining the Foundations

*I*t is not easy to get good results, and when we talk about results we do not only think of SAT scores. To get into a good college you also need good results in high school courses. You need to accept the challenge and take the more difficult courses your school offers.

"Colleges love to see that kids accept challenges," the guidance counselor repeated over and over. I looked at my wife and we wondered how to explain to her that being in high school was already a challenge for our daughter. How to explain to her that in the last years we had to move twice, that our cardboard boxes and ourselves were getting old, that to straighten our daughter's teeth we had to wait for years and do it much later than the others, that we were finally able to open a new credit and pay for it so our daughter too could look at the world with a beautiful smile, with the self-confidence of the one who knows that life is beautiful and it belongs to him.

For many years we made many sacrifices to help our children build their future in this our new country. Every book bought to give them the foundations to get better results was also building up their confidence. But they tried to destroy the self-confidence that our kids had built up step by step, not intentionally, of course; whenever people hurt others they hurt them unintentionally.

When our daughter got a distinction for her PSAT scores, the second PSAT, the one that every eleventh grader in the USA must take, we hugged her and repeated to her how much this distinction meant because we have read in the books that described what the good colleges looked for in a student, that the applications asked for a list of awards and recognitions. Nonetheless, someone in school told her that the PSAT didn't count; that what was really important was the SAT.

False, the PSAT counted. Both the first and the second PSAT counted as practice for the SAT if they were taken as a challenge and not only as a diagnostic test. Even more, the best universities look at everything. The College Board, the organization that administers these tests, sends the scores from the second PSAT to colleges.

Four months before the mandatory PSAT, in May of her sophomore year, our daughter took her first SAT for college. That gave her the possibility to take it three times until she got a score of 1500 out of the possible 1600; not the first, not the second but the third time, and still with time to take the test a fourth time if necessary. That gave her enough time to prepare for the three SAT II subject tests. She took Math and French in May, and English in June, all that in her junior year. Knowing that she still had time ahead allowed her to take the tests without so much stress.

In March of our daughter's junior year she asked for the applications to the colleges of her choice, and completed them. She wanted to know what those colleges were looking for in a candidate, how she compared to that profile, and what was still needed in order to make her stand out among the pool of applicants so as to secure, as much as she could, her admission. She wanted to put all the stakes on her side.

We saw that they asked for two letters of recommendation. Our daughter chose two teachers, one from the humanities and social sciences and one from the math and sciences area, and asked them for recommendations. To make sure that their letters included information beyond the strictly academic, she prepared a sheet with the information she thought the teachers needed to give the admissions committees a comprehensive image of herself: her accomplishments, her sacrifices to get were she was, what she had not been able to do because of a lack of money, her dreams and aspirations.

Since she knew for sure the college she wanted to attend, she decided to apply early admission, which meant applying in October of her senior year, so as to get the answer in December. This implied having all the scores in hand before fall. Applying this way binds the student to attend that college if accepted. "The worst-case scenario is that I am not accepted,' thought our daughter, 'and in that case I will still have time to send applications to other colleges. I have nothing to lose."

"As you can see,' she added 'you do not have four years, but three. You can wait, but that gives you less time to improve your scores if necessary. I prefer to think that senior year does not exist, that it is a kind of spare wheel to use only in case of emergency."

When she got the 1500 one of her classmates told her: "The SAT is for idiots, it doesn't measure intelligence and it doesn't have any interest. I do not get better results because I am too smart and I am not able to think at such a low level, but now I am aware of that, and the next time I will get a perfect score."

And our daughter continued smiling to hide her pain. As in eighth grade, they had stolen her triumph. They wanted to ignore her accomplishments; it seemed that the results were a proof of success depending on the color of your skin.

In the case of our son the arguments were different. Since they couldn't deny his grades they spoke behind his back, and said: "He has no life, he doesn't sleep; once he stayed three days and three nights without eating or sleeping just to study for a test!" And in front of him they said: "I don't get good grades because I don't study, if I studied no one would beat me. I am a natural and get decent results without killing myself. You instead need to study night and day." No one wanted to recognize that he studied; studying was bad, it meant being an idiot, it was not cool.

The rumors about our son were so bad that one day in the supermarket, the mother of one of our son's classmates (one of the girls that had stayed behind), a woman a little bit more than middle aged told us: "I can't wait for the day when I see your son sweat his guts out." The mother of one of our daughter's classmates who was listening added, "Me either." Only then and there we understood the huge pressure that our children carried on their shoulders.

To make them feel bad, they looked at their clothes, talked about their next vacations, or the new video game our children didn't have. Or, when the moment to visit colleges arrived, they used to tell them: "This weekend we are going to visit colleges, which one are you going to visit?" And at home we were browsing catalogs, in the friendly bookstore we studied what the colleges were asking for, and silently, almost in secret, we looked at the prices.

Our children saw their right to feel successful, to be successful, denied. They were denied the sweaty taste of triumph, of belonging. They had to make them feel different, useless, those poor foreigners who are not from here, and dare to fight and leave their place!

The Finish Line at Our Reach

The awaited moment was here, the moment to choose a college, and with luck, the college of your dreams would choose you. The school organized a general meeting with parents, and then individual meetings of parents and children with the guidance counselors.

We arrived to the meeting with hopes and expectations, knowing that we had everything on our side. We didn't get to the meeting empty handed; we knew that the guidance counselors alone could not make miracles happen, that getting your child into college is a joint effort from parents, kids and school. Working together is the key to success.

Our daughter had prepared herself. During the four years of high school she took the most challenging courses offered by the school and managed to keep a very high GPA, she took the SAT I and got 1500 on her third try, she had accumulated a few honors and national recognitions for her academic achievements, and she had some extracurricular activities and community service. Her goal was to get into a high competitive university. "Nowadays', she used to tell us, 'when you look for a job, they not only see that you have a college degree, they also see where you got that degree."

She had also browsed college catalogs and decided on the "school of her dreams," had made a short list of other schools that she also liked, and looked at their application forms to make sure that she had all the tests these schools required.

The guidance counselor did some research too, thinking of what she believed were the best bets for our daughter to get into college. She, better than anyone else, knew how competitive the entrance to college had become in the last years. "I have just come back from a small university in the mountains of the southern United States," started the counselor. "It has a beautiful campus, tranquil, far from the city. It is not a renowned university, I know, but I spoke to the director of admissions about your daughter and he exclaimed that she was the kind of student that they were looking for. We found the perfect match for you," she said looking at our daughter.

The three of us looked at the floor and we saw, spread all over all her accomplishments, years and years of sacrifice going down the drain. We could hear the silence, the same heavy silence that years before we heard when the teachers of the junior high told us that there were special courses for kids with "learning disabilities," like ours, but that it had to be our decision to send them there.

My wife and I kept silent; this time it was our daughter who spoke, "No, thank you." She handed her copy of the information sheet she had prepared for the teachers who were going to recommend her, and in a tone each time more sure she added, "This information is to be used to complete the portion of the application that the school needs to fill out. I want to attend Columbia University."

The guidance counselor looked at our daughter and in a technical language, she said, "We can consider that university as a reach. That means that your chances of being accepted there are slight; none of the students from our school have been accepted there for the last ten years." And she suggested several other universities. Because of her years of experience, she knew that our daughter's goal was very difficult to reach. She was afraid for her, that she could be disappointed if she did not get in.

"We'll make a list of five universities starting with the safe ones." She wrote the names on a piece of paper and Columbia didn't figure in the list.

"Columbia is my first choice," said our daughter. "Ever since eighth grade I have wanted to go there." We looked at her curiously. She had kept that secret to herself until we went to visit Columbia. Yes, we too went to visit colleges. To tell the truth, Columbia was the only campus we visited because it was close to us. The summer of her senior year we called, asked about the campus tours, asked permission from our jobs and went to visit. From our first step on campus we loved it. It was located within the limits of two worlds, the city of New York and a popular neighborhood that sheltered the homes of many of ours.

The gardens, playgrounds for kids of the neighborhood and students were protected by the shade of the immense library, and the curricula sounded universal. Our kids got lost going from building to building, and my wife and I went to talk to the people of financial aid and tell them that we could not to afford to send our daughter there without financial aid. They invited us to an informational meeting that luckily took place on a holiday.

As every parent we wanted to give to this visit the character of a party, so we invited our children to eat at *El rey del pollo frito/The Fried Chicken King,* and sitting at its humble tables we ate chicken legs served with yellow rice. At the table beside ours was sitting the director of admissions and his secretary. We thought that to be a good sign.

The day of the informational meeting there were food and beverages and it gave us the opportunity to talk with other parents and our daughter to talk with other students interested in applying to Columbia. The meeting started with the speech of an alumna who despite her scarce means had reached her goals of studying there. We were so happy! She explained how she had taken advantage of her life in the City for her personal growth, how what she had learned in the streets, the free concerts, and the free exhibits had enriched what she studied in the classroom. She mentioned, without advising anyone to do it, how she took the risk to apply to only one college.

After her spoke a guy who won every kid's sympathy by saying that they didn't have to worry so much about numbers, scores, SAT Is or SAT IIs. "To tell you the truth,' he finished, 'no one cares about those numbers."

The Dean of Admissions took the microphone and said, "I care, and the admissions committee cares. The scores on the SAT I and II, the GPA and the strength of the academic program give us evidence of the student's academic record, as well as his determination to accept and face challenges." In silence I thought, "I care too; I knew it; I was not wrong."

Most of the parents' questions dealt with financial issues, and the Dean said: "The kids we accept here all deserve to be here, they have won their spot here based on their merits. If we accept them it is because they are the best, and we will do whatever we can to help them come." We loved that man!

When the guidance counselor saw our daughter's determination she told her, "Apply to Columbia, we will keep the list I prepared on hand, just in case."

Our daughter smiled, my wife and I were able to breathe again. The road to the finish line was being cleared of obstacles.

Affirmative Action

When our daughter mentioned at school what college she planned to apply to her classmates glanced at each other and one of them said, "You will get in for sure because you are not from here."

True, we are not from here, but at the same time we are, and our children are not taking anyone's place.

If there's a program to help the ones who need it to get into colleges it is because they need some help today so that tomorrow their children and the children of their children do not need of that help and can go all their way in equal conditions and with the same advantages as everyone else. It is not the color of the skin that is unequal; it is the system that is unfair, and that's the reason why Affirmative Action, the program that offers this help exists.

No one raises his voice when students get into college in part because they are good athletes; no one raises his voice when students are given legacy privileges. But when it has to do with an ethnic minority people get upset and make you feel it is a charity, as if you were allowed to be where you do not belong, just as a favor.

They make our children feel unwelcome, so on edge that many of these kids give up. The pressure against the ones that dare to leave the place they were assigned is huge. They want us to remain the way they see us, poor, lazy, uneducated.

They do not want us to belong. They can help us get to a good college, but always reminding us that we do not really belong but rather are there as a favor. They make us feel that we are taking somebody else's place even if that is not true. That way they marginalize us, and they push us to quit. Affirmative action should not only help us to get there, but also affirm our pride and self-confidence.

How can we make the Deans of Admissions in colleges understand that it is not enough to accept our children into their programs, that colleges must strive to make them feel welcome, to reassure them that they were accepted because of their merits, which give them the right to be there. They must prevent them from being isolated or from isolating themselves; their voices must be heard, and the colleges should provide for their voices to be heard.

The words "You will be accepted, you are not from here, you are a Latina" resounded in our daughter's ears as an insult. When she told us about that we explained to her how we saw the role of Affirmative Action. We told her that there is nothing wrong with being part of a minority, and that we are very proud of being Latinos. We also told her that if she got into a very good university it was not because she was a Latina, but because of all that she was, including being a Latina, because of her work, her achievements, and her and our sacrifices. And though it was true that we owed the bank a lot of money, she didn't owe anyone anything because she had walked on her own the long way to the door that would lead her to her dreams of a better life.

We also told her that even though with her grades and test scores she didn't need that program to be accepted at a good college, she had to support it thinking of our people, thinking of the ones that still needed a hand to get farther; that she had to stand for it because it's purpose is to rectify an injustice, and that she should not be ashamed of fighting injustice.

If we are not capable of saying "I am," they will never allow us to be. We are not asking to be accepted as a favor; we are simply asking that our values be recognized. Never ask to be accepted, you have to make yourself accepted by showing your values and merits. "The road has two ends, and both we and they must walk towards the middle," we told our daughter.

The Application

*I*n October of her senior year we had to start filling out college applications. From the box labeled *universidad* we took out the rough drafts of the applications our daughter had completed in summer before her junior year, as well as the honors and distinctions earned through so much pain.

We asked for new application packages from the one college our daughter wanted to attend. Without telling her we asked for other application forms to colleges that she could attend in the event she was not accepted in the one of her choice.

We had asked the Dean of Admissions and the Director of Financial Aid at Columbia, "What happens if you accept her and we don't have the resources to send our daughter here?" And they had answered "That is not an issue, if she is accepted the college will do anything to get her here." In that situation, we told ourselves, "Why not? Let's tempt the devil," as we say in our countries.

As soon as we received the application package we sat at our old table and read it over and over to make sure that we would not miss anything. Putting together the first application package became a family moment, a beautiful moment. We made our daughter feel that although she was leaving home she was not alone, that we supported her decision and were profoundly proud of her.

She took a sheet of paper and started to write down, for a second time, what they were asking for. She didn't want to write anything on the official papers until being sure that she had everything right.

Honors and Awards: It is a great honor to be here, at this point, my wife and I told to ourselves chuckling, but that certificate signed *mami* and *papi* was not on the list of examples of honors that the school had given to us. Instead the *commended student* for her scores in the PSAT (test that a classmate had told her didn't count) was on the list, and she included it.

In those same days we received notification that our daughter had merited an honor certificate from the *National Hispanic Recognition Program* that recognizes Hispanic students for their excellent score on the same test, score that placed her among the Hispanic students with the highest scores in the nation. She proudly added it to the list. It was a national award that recognized her as a "scholar," the highest distinction, one of the top students of the list.

She was not able to include the awards that

she was handed in the parking lot or in the classroom in junior high, but they were in her heart, and in a way they showed up.

There was a section for extracurricular activities and community service. We had found out about that in freshman year when our daughter told us one day how important it was to have them when applying for college. Without being completely sure of what she meant, we had told her, "We guess that it should be like with the kids who intend to get into college for sports. It is better to concentrate on one and excel in it than to practice a different sport every season without standing out in any. By finding ways to practice the one of their choice all year long they will show commitment, determination, and improvement. That can make the difference because that is what the future coach in college will be looking for.

For us it is the same. Since we do not have a lot of financial means or time, we must balance everything without neglecting the grades, and the preparation for the required tests. It is better to show consistency in doing one or two extracurricular activities well, to show a clear commitment towards something than to fly from flower to flower as a hummingbird who disappears without leaving traces."

Our daughter filled out fewer lines in that section of the application, but those few lines showed her commitment, consistency and determination in life. All that played in her favor; her application was a coherent whole.

Her hand shaking with emotion but firm

with determination she completed the section for the scores on the tests: SAT I, SAT II, GPA.

She compared those numbers with the results of the students that had been accepted in that university the previous year to verify what her real chances of being accepted were. That allowed her to see how her hard work had helped her approach her goal.

We had come from so far; from a sleepless night in the South of the United States when we decided to stake all on the future of our children, from being literally hungry, but still eating "all you can" in books and study. We were coming from the very bottom, that place that everyone despises; we were part of that group that is always ignored, that is never greeted or welcomed, that has to cede to others a parking spot. We the underdogs were giving our children the possibility to dream.

Every line of the application completed represented a hope, every line was perceived as a possibility of winning. When she had finished our daughter told us, "They ask for an essay, what can I write about? The children from the wealthy neighborhood talk about paid charity trips to go build schools in third world countries, trips to Europe to learn a foreign language, and I..." And she kept silent; she didn't want to make us feel sad.

Her mother hugged her and almost crying told her, "Talk about yourself, my daughter, of the sacrifices you have endured to be were you are, of the things you were unable to accomplish because of a lack of money, of your dreams and aspirations. This is your sole opportunity to "talk" to the admissions committee and let them know and appreciate who you really are.

The next morning she read her essay to us. It talked about who she was, about the difficulties of being, about her origins, her untiring search for a place in this world, for the rights of the have-nots, and while listening to her so many visions came to our minds.

As it was a habit in the school, she gave the essay to her English teacher to read. Around three days later he handed it back to her. With a gloomy face she told us, "The teacher says that my essay is not a conventional essay, that it is not what the admission people expect, that it is beautiful but that I have to write something more conventional, that essays have another kind of structure."

"Your essay is different, the teacher is paying you homage," we told her. "Sign it and send it." She put the package together and sent it. We were in October, and the catalog said that we should expect an answer by December 15.

"Two and a half months of agony, I'm going to die," our daughter told us. Two and a half months? You forgot how to count, my daughter; the wait had started years ago, when you first set step in a small rural school in Georgia.

The Mailman Rang Twice

On December 15 we asked for a half-day off, we wanted to be home when the mailman arrived so we would be able to take the answer to our daughter in school. The previous night nobody slept.

Our daughter had told us that there were two different kinds of envelopes, a small one that contained a sheet folded in three and which letter started with the words "We regret to inform you..." And a big one with several papers, a course catalog, and a letter that started with "We are pleased to inform you..." Regardless of the envelope, she asked us not to open it and bring it to school, that she would be allowed to pick it up at the counselors' office.

When we arrived home at one o'clock the mailman had already delivered our mail. In the mailbox we didn't see any big envelope. Infinitely sad we took out the mail looking for the small envelope, but nothing. As usual we found bills, as usual advertising newspapers offering things that we didn't need, as usual letters from companies offering more and more credit cards, as if we didn't have too many already, but nothing from Columbia.

We ran to the refrigerator to check our calendar and make sure that the date was December 15, but we were not mistaken, it was clearly stated that December 15 was the date for the answer.

When we went to pick up our children our daughter was already waiting outside. We had never seen her so helpless and appalled. She walked to the car, looked at us, and only inside she dared to ask with a little voice: "Why are you so sad? We got the small envelope, didn't we?"

"Something happened," we told her. "We didn't get any answer. There's probably a delay."

The other kids that had applied early admission had all received their letters. As the day went by all the parents arrived at the school to bring them the news. It seems that every parent had made the same promise, not to open the envelope and bring it to the school immediately.

Never before had dinnertime been so depressing. We were unable to understand why we had not received any letter. It is outrageous, we thought, that they have not even answered.

Almost by the end of dinner we heard the doorbell ring, it was the employee of one of those private companies that deliver special mail. He told us that he came by in the morning but since there was nobody home he decided to come back in the evening before returning the truck to the garage. He opened his bag and took out an envelope. It was a big one.

The poor man couldn't understand why we were screaming so loud and hugging each other crying. Our daughter opened the envelope and among all the papers she took out a sticker that said "Columbia University."

The sun was almost gone when we walked to our car and put the sticker on the rear window, as all the other parents and kids. We then took a step back and looked at it with pride.

The next day we drove around town at five miles an hour, so everyone could see the sticker greeting proudly other parents that were driving at the same speed.

In the months that followed the scholarships started to arrive, the ones that were merit based, the ones that were need based. The first thing we did was to go online and fill out the FAFSA (Free Application for Federal Student Aid) to find out the scholarships and federal grants our daughter qualified for. The first one was the "Gates Millennium Scholars." Bill Gates and his wife Melissa had established a scholarship program for minorities. The students who qualify get the money to pay whatever the difference is between the financial aid package granted by the college of their choice and the college's tuition fees.

A friend told us about the "Hispanic Scholarship Fund," an organization that grants scholarships to Hispanic students. On their website we also found a long list of other scholarships intended also for our children. We also looked for general scholarships, and chose from the list the ones to which our daughter qualified to apply. We took note of the deadlines, downloaded the application forms, and filled them out systematically. We didn't want to arrive with empty pockets; it was a matter of pride, but it was also to make sure that our daughter could attend the college of her choice. The University kept its promise, and our daughter was ready to attend Columbia.

Yes, when they want a student they do anything to help him go, and by the way, they told us they had loved our daughter's essay because it was different, authentic, non conventional.

That summer flew by. We had a new list in our hands, but this time it was a different kind of list: a couple of sheets, a couple of towels, a suitcase (a suitcase, not a cardboard box), a big dictionary, notebooks, pencils and *The Odyssey*. Yes, they had asked her to read *The Odyssey*. "Which one?" We asked our daughter laughing.

Crossing The Finish Line

The day we left our daughter in what is reputed to be one of the best universities in the United States, I had the vision of the small chubby little girl that, with a smile on her face, urged me to pick her up in my arms so she could climb on my shoulders to look far away into the distance; first she, and later on her brother. And when they got tired they both leaned their heads over mine to fall asleep and dream, their eyes wide open lost in the horizon.

Today, I was watching her as she disappeared into the crowd of newly arrived students, and from the corner of a square, turn her head over to us and smile. Her eyes shining with silent tears she told us "¡Gracias! Thank you!" And then continued walking steadfastly, self-confidently. She was and belonged at Columbia University, and she knew it.

Coming back home in our old car we cried of sadness; she was the first one to leave home. We also cried of happiness for her success.

We were getting out of the tunnel that connects New York to New Jersey when we heard the voice of our son from behind that said, "I want to go to Harvard."

Our daughter's successful experience had given him even more confidence. "My sister was right, 'you do not have four years, but three' to get ready for college," he said referring to why he had already decided to take the first SAT in his sophomore year, scoring 1420, and for a second time in junior year, right after taking the PSAT, scoring1550.

My wife and I looked at each other and thought, "We hit the jackpot! This time we will be condemned to a diet of bread and water for a month."

At that moment we saw our dream of owning a house definitely going down the drain. We knew that in three more years, once our son finished high school we had to leave the town where we were living if we wanted to start paying our debts, and that once again we would be loading our old cardboard boxes, but this time without the children counting *una, dos, tres...*

True, we will not, but our children and our children's children will be able to live where they want to, in the town they choose, fulfilling their dreams. My daughter, my son, yours will be the opportunity in this land of opportunities.

We looked into the car's rear-view-mirror once more to see where we were coming from, after which we sped away, not having much time left. We still had one more to go, and the road was not downhill, but rather it ascended, without limits.

The Landmarks Along the Road

Our Daughter	The normal path + what worked for our kids	Check
Grade: 7 & 8		√
Sat I: She qualified to take it as part of the Talent Search Program sponsored by the Johns Hopkins University (January)	Sat I: at this point, the test serves as a diagnostic exam. Furthermore, the more a student practices, the better his/her results. It is not necessary to qualify, you can register directly @ www.collegeboard.com (Register in November to take the test in January)	
Grade: 9		
Starting in ninth grade, and all through her four high school years she took several honor and AP courses.	Take as many honor or AP courses as you can. Colleges look at your GPA, but also at the strength of the academic program you followed. It shows them your determination in accepting and facing challenges. If your high school does not offer honor or AP courses, make that stand out in your application.	
	Find out what extra-curricular activities are good for you. Colleges prefer to see few activities, but considerable involvement. They also want to see constancy, commitment, motivation, service to others, and leadership.	

Grade: 10		
PSAT (The school offered it as a practice) (October)	*PSAT (voluntary: ask your counselor how to register)* *(October)*	
SAT I: First try (May)		
Summer before Junior year. She completed the application to the College she intended to apply as a rough draft to determine what this college was looking for in an applicant, and how she could enhance her chances to be admitted.	**Summer before Junior year**: *Complete a mock application to one of the Colleges you would like to apply.* *You can register at the College Board web site www.collegeboard.com where you can get the profiles of the colleges of your choice. Download the application from "admissions" at the College of your choice's web site.* In **September** give a copy of the essay that will accompany this application to your English teacher for review and feedback. Give a copy of the application to your guidance counselor to give him/her an idea of what you want, and where you stand so he/she can give you advice.	
Grade: 11		
	Begin preparation for the PSAT. Complete a section of each part per weekend, and a full PSAT the 4th weekend. (September)	

PSAT: mandatory (October)	PSAT: mandatory (October) *Begin preparation for the SAT immediately after taking the PSAT. The first month, complete a section of each part every weekend.* *The second month, two sections of each part every weekend.* *The third month (December) a full SAT every weekend.*	
	Meet with your guidance counselor to get feedback on your mock application and to discuss your choices and possibilities. (November)	
SAT I: Second try (January)	*SAT I or ACT: First try after the PSAT.* *Check which one of the two tests the colleges you're looking at require.* (January)	
SAT II: (Columbia University required three) (she took two in May and one in June)	*SAT I or ACT or SAT II* *Check which tests the colleges you are interested in require. Highly competitive colleges usually ask for three SAT IIs.* (May and June)	
At the end of her junior year she asked two of her teachers (one in the Humanities and Social Sciences area and one in the Math and Sciences) for letters of recommendation. She provided them with an outline that contained what she	*Ask two of your teachers (one in the Humanities and Social Sciences area and one in the Math and Sciences) for letters of recommendation.* *Provide them with information on what you consider is important for them to include in the*	

considered was important for them to include in their letters: her achievements, the sacrifices she made to get where she was, and what she had not been able to do as a result of a lack of money. (June)	*letter that does not necessarily show up on your high school transcript: accomplishments, sacrifices you have made to get where you are, and what you had not been able to do as a result of financial constraints. The letters of recommendation should provide the admissions committee with a comprehensive image of the applicant including his/her academic and extracurricular accomplishments, character, and potential to succeed in College.* (June)
	Write the essay that will accompany your application during the summer. Remember: every person is unique. Look for that particular trait that will make you stand out among the pool of applicants. The essay is your opportunity to actually "talk" to the admissions committee. **(Summer before your Senior year)**
Grade: 12	
She gave the same information to her guidance counselor for when she had to complete certain portions of the college application form. (June)	*Give your guidance counselor the same information you gave to your teachers, so that he/she can complete the portions of your application that require his/her input.* (June)
	Give a copy of your college essay to one or two English teachers for review and feedback. (September)

	Apply for the FAFSA PIN (Personal Identification Number) @ : www.pin.ed.gov You will need it to fill out the FAFSA (Free Application for Federal Student Aid). It takes from 7 to 10 days to get it by mail, 3 days via e-mail (December)
Completed the FAFSA (January)	***To apply for Financial Aid, complete the FAFSA @ www.fafsa.ed.gov*** (January) Deadline: June 30. Deadline to make corrections online: August 15
She applied *early decision* to Columbia University. She also filled out four other applications to "possible" colleges in case she was deferred or rejected. (October)	*If you are sure of the college you want to attend, apply early decision or early action.* *Early decision is binding, which means that you have to go to this college if accepted; early action is not binding, you have until March to decide whether you will attend this college or not. Advantage: you have time to compare financial aid packages offered to you by the different colleges.* *Have other applications ready, just in case.* *The deadline to send early decision or early action application packages is usually* Oct. 15. Decision letter Dec.15

	Start putting together the regular admission application packages (October or November) The deadline to send regular admission application packages is generally between January 10th and 15th.	
SAT I: Third and last try. Score 1500. (October)	SAT I/ACT or SAT II if still needed (October-November-January)	
Accepted to Columbia University (December 15)		
	Admission decisions mailed to regular decision applicants: (March or April)	

Remember that there is not a single, solely correct way of achieving a goal, and that different paths can lead to the same end.

Remember that who you really are and what you will bring to the college of your choice is much more important than test scores. Diversity (racial, economical, religious or other) leadership, a different perspective of life, and the role model that you will represent after college for those left behind are essential parts of your being cherished at any higher education institution.

Keep in mind that if you start late, the solution is not to panic, but to speed up, to turn off the TV and accelerate, remembering that in order to succeed and have a better life you must work hard and put everything on your side.

Free Online SAT Preparation

As previously mentioned, one of the keys to success is to have a head start in the race for college. The web provides you with countless sources of free preparation practice. Below are a few that were useful to us. Some of them give you a specific question every day to help you stay in shape. Others provide you with timed tests to round off your training.

Remember, there are no miracles; the secret lies in an early start. Our advice is practice, practice, and practice.

www.number2.com
www.kaptest.com
www.takesat.com
www.freesat1prep.com
www.gomath.com
www.doyourmath.com
www.4tests.com
www.myessay.com
www.studyhall.com
www.collegeboard.com

Financial Aid: Scholarships

The first thing to do in December of the student's senior year is to apply for the FAFSA PIN (personal identification number) @ www.pin.ed.gov in order to fill out the FAFSA (www.fafsa.ed.gov), a governmental form used to determine eligibility to receive federal aid, and to calculate the family's expected contribution. The FAFSA (Free Application for Federal Student Aid) is also used by colleges to determine the financial aid package they offer based on need.

Probably the most appealing scholarship for Hispanic Americans, African Americans, American Indians, Alaska Natives, and Asian Pacific Islanders is the "Gates Millennium Scholars Program" www.gmsp.org. Eligibility for this scholarship is based on the applicant's GPA, which must be above a 3.3 on a scale of 4.0 (82.5 on a scale of 100) and his or her leadership qualities and service to the community. In addition, applicants must be eligible to receive a Federal Pell Grant, which is determined by the FAFSA according to income, the size of the candidate's family, and the number of students in the family. The application can be found on-line; contenders must be nominated by a principal, a counselor, or a teacher.

We learned from experience that one must keep a calendar with scholarship deadlines clearly marked. It is very easy to lose scholarship opportunities for the simple reason of missing a deadline. For instance, the deadline for the "Gates" scholarship is in mid January, whereas for the Hispanic National Fund it is in mid October. It is wise to mark two dates for each scholarship, the deadline, and a date around a month and a half prior the deadline to commence filling out the application with ample time.

Since no one can guarantee that you get a certain scholarship you must explore other options. In our case we found the following sites very useful:

www.finaid.org
www.finaid.org/otheraid/minority.phtml
www.finaid.org/otheraid/female.phtml
www.hispanicscholarships.com
www.gmsp.org (GATES)
www.aspira.org
www.laef.org

Another sensible thing to do is to look for all the scholarships that fit the student's profile, and not exclusively for scholarships for minorities. You can look by state, by college, by gender, by careers, etc.

For example, the College Board has a database of 2,300 scholarships (federal, state, public and private); Fastweb and Collegenet have a database of 600,000. These lists are updated on a regular basis.

www.collegeboard.com
www.fastweb.com
www.collegenet.com/mach25
www.scholarships101.com
www.wiredscholars.com
www.scholarships.com
www.scholarships-now.com
www.finaid.org/otheraid/sports.phtml
www.guaranteedscholarships.com
www.scholarshipsarus.org/athletic.htm
www.uncf.org
www.invent.org/collegiate/
www.edu.gov/index.jhtml
www.apsanet.org/PS/grants/aspen3.cfm
www.project-excellence.com
www.rotary.org/programs/ambscho

Completing an application takes time, but it yields results that regardless of the amount will help clear the road to college.

Scholarships can range from only a few hundred to thousands of dollars, and in the end, any amount of money justifies the time invested.

If you are denied a scholarship, you waste nothing but a bit of your time, and that is far preferable to living with doubts and regrets about what *could have* been had you applied.

Also by
Ediciones Nuevo Espacio / www.editorial-ene.com

Yo, Alejandro, English, Third Edition, 1-930879-21-0 reviewed in *Booklist Magazine*, ALA (American Library Association).
"Completing this, his first book, before his twelfth birthday is only one of Alejandro's impressive personal conquests. Sharing his innocent observations with a staggeringly rich vocabulary, he relates two primary objectives: to fit in with but stand out among his peers and to win the respect of his teachers...
Alejandro's observations are sharp, and his writing style is endearingly rustic.
...a promising young talent who has written a book worth savoring, even by readers older than the target age group."
Roger Leslie,
Booklist, March 1, 2001

Yo, Alejandro reviewed in *Journal of Adolescent &Adult Literacy*, International Reading Association Society's greatest assets are its children because within them rest the hopes and aspirations for an ever changing and improving future. Why is it then that society insists on plaguing its prized possessions with the injustices of racism and discrimination?

Yo, Alejandro is the autobiographical tale of a 12-year-old Latino coping with the pressures of belonging to an ethnic minority in the United States. It provides insight to many important social and cultural questions. Born into a world that categorizes people according to ethnicity, Alejandro Gac-Artigas is presented with a difficult journey at the outset of his life: overcoming the prejudices of society. He shares with the reader many experi.ences that have opened his eyes to the ways of the world.

A newcomer to the USA, Alejandro arrives in Georgia from Puerto Rico without knowing how to speak English. He is placed in Campus Daycare where he experiences firsthand the bittersweet taste of American culture. Initially, Alejandro's struggles are similar to those of most children — learning how to ride a bicycle, making friends, playing the piano, and doing well at school. However, as he grows older Alejandro is introduced to an entirely new set of problems that seem at first glance trivial but prove to be instrumental in his psychological development and maturation.

Through short excerpts, Alejandro describes his realization of the pettiness and jealousy of adults, the hypocrisy of the law, the pains of separation, the inherent materialism in society, and the overwhelming problem of racism in America. In working through these numerous obstacles, he rises about social conventions to demonstrate that even the impossible is possible.

The most striking aspect of this novel is that it was written by a 12-year-old. I was pleasantly surprised by the way this young author conveyed powerful messages of love, friendship, and courage.

I applaud Alejandro for taking the initiative to launch such a huge endeavor and commend his ability to express himself eloquently. Alejandro introduces a plethora of social issues for discussion, focusing primarily on racism and prejudice. He innocently questions the reasoning for such narrow-minded worldviews and attempts to prove their illogicality by sharing his accomplishments in light of all the obstacles that hinder his success.

Alejandro understands that his life is not all bad and that he is blessed to be surrounded by a loving family and several caring friends, but he.also knows that so much more awaits him. Alejandro's ability to appreciate his own personal triumphs makes this story all the more appealing. His book is an impressive example of the power of the human spirit.

I would recommend this novel for older children who would be able to discern the importance of Alejandro's story. It is necessary for young people to become aware of the social issues inherent in modern culture and to discuss them openly. The book provides an ideal forum for debate and the opportunity to reveal aspects of society that may otherwise remain obscured.

Iva Vukin,
December 2001-January 2002
International Reading Association

Yo, Alejandro reviewed in *Promise*, the newsletter of the New Jersey Association for Gifted Children

Yo, Alejandro is such a tale of poignancy. Twelve year old Alejandro recounts with youthful tenderness his struggles as a young Latino boy trying to find acceptance in the Unites States without sacrificing his cultural heritage. For one so young, he captures the painful and illogical essence of prejudice. Alejandro's tale is not one of defeat. His book tells how he achieves success, finds acceptance as an advanced student, and uses his sorrow to promote equality not hate.

Yo, Alejandro... is a book worth sharing. This young boy is certainly a gifted writer whose work can serve as a model for other children and can be used to promote cultural acceptance. His message to let the people know his story, so that it doesn't happen again is well delivered.

I recently shared it with some of my students. The lively discussion that it provoked reminded me that sometimes children see the world far more clear than adults!

Patti Coughlan.
Promise, the newsletter of the New Jersey Association for Gifted Children, vol. 9 no. 4 spring 2001

Teachers

I absolutely loved the book. I found it to be wonderfully poignant, descriptive and Alejandro's life experiences contained therein seem to swim straight into the hearts and souls of all who read this book

Darcy Whitte, Assistant Principal
Pegasus Charter School, Dallas, Texas

The students thought you were excellent; in fact, they thought you were AWESOME!! I am glad you touched [their] hearts and opened their minds to be respectful and considerate of others regardless of their race, color, or religion. Alejandro, you have a lot to offer to the world with your expressive and poetic words and personality. I am certain you will be successful.

Todd Pisani, Teacher of Spanish
Marlboro Middle School. NJ.

Writing a book is a terrific accomplishment for any young man! Also, you are wonderful model for our bilingual students!

Katherine Cooner, Teacher of ESL,
Ocean Township Intermediate School, NJ

You are an inspiration for the Bradley children!

Fran Green
Bradley Elementary School, Asbury Park, NJ

Alejandro, you have a spirit of forgiveness that will take you far. Not looking back but ahead with a positive force is a gift. Thank you for teaching me. You point out a valuable message.

Mrs. Kubaitis
Knollwood School, Fair Haven, NJ.

Alejandro, you recall your childhood experiences in a voice that is at once innocent and wise. Thank you for sharing your wisdom with me.

Vanessa Kabash
Knollwood School, Fair Haven, NJ

Students

You manage to inspire me in ways that no other young man could. Your hard work and dedication are a driving force in this world. And hopefully your message will spread like a brush fire.

Navid Faryar, 8 grade, Knollwood
Fair Haven, NJ

As you, I also came to this country when I was three. I knew no English and had to learn English through the TV. I think your book was very inspirational.
Your book not only showed kids that they are not alone, but it broke the boundary. You showed the world that kids can write and print a book, not just adults. I think it's quite amazing that at your age you wrote and published a book, and you are still working on ANOTHER!

Vivian Nguyen
Marlboro Middle School, NJ

I can understand what you went through. My mother and I went through similar things, her being Cuban and me being half Cuban. It's amazing how cruel people can be when they mean it as a joke.

Eva San Martin
Marlboro Middle School, NJ

I think it's great what you did. You have inspired me to keep a diary.

Sofia
Marlboro Middle School, NJ

I think it would be good if people will change from reading your book.

Erica
Marlboro Middle School, NJ

I bought your book and you are my favorite writer in the world.

Alberto
Marlboro Middle School, NJ

I am from Ghana, Africa. I liked your first book because I felt the same thing you felt when you came here.

Anita Opoku-Darico
Ocean Township Middle School, NJ.

Another book by Alejandro Gac-Artigas:
Off to Catch the Sun
Collection of poems and short stories 1-930879-28-8
Following his poignant, breakthrough auto-biography, *Yo, Alejandro* (2000), Gac-Artigas (now 13) tackles both short fiction and poetry in this erudite, impressively literary collection. In the first half of the book, essays and reflections thinly veiled as short stories capture the heart of narrators who struggle with homelessness, futility, and even McCarthyism. The poetry that follows is an exploration of styles and themes that work as well in both versions of childhood fable ("Beanstalk and the Jack") and in more mature, sometimes comically mangled verse. Gac-Artigas' rich literary background should impress both young readers (especially in "Rumphus Rue" his tribute to Shel Silverstein) and teachers (his adroit emulation of Ernest Hemingway's narrator, Robert Jordan, from *For Whom the Bell Tolls*). Even when his experimentation with language is craggy, readers will marvel at his fearless attempts to express in vivid metaphor ideas that would normally be far beyond the scope of someone yet to reach his teens.

Roger Leslie
Booklist. 2001

Alejandro Gac-Artigas was born in the Netherlands on October 22, 1988, and moved to the United States in July 1991. His father is from Chile and his mother from Puerto Rico.

In November 2000 he published his first book, ***Yo, Alejandro***, that he completed a month before his 12th birthday. In March 2003, a bilingual edition of the book appeared under the title: ***Yo, Alejandro, my/our Story*** (*Yo, Alejandro, mi/nuestra historia*).

In September 2001 he published a second book: ***Off to Catch the Sun***, a collection of short stories and poems.

Speaker and workshop leader in different state conferences in NY; in schools in Monmouth county, NJ, where he lives as well as in the state of Texas; in university programs addressed to minority groups; and for National Institutions that fight against racism and discrimination in our communities and society.

Awards and Recognitions
National Honor Society - French Honor Society
Scholar of the National Hispanic Recognition Program for the scores in the PSAT - Candidate to Commended (or Semifinalist) of the National Merit Scholarship Program
Certificate of Accomplishment awarded by Princeton University: **The Princeton Prize in Race Relations 2004** "to promote harmony, respect, and understanding among people of different races by identifying and recognizing high school age students whose efforts have had a significant, positive effect on race relations in their schools or communities." May 2004.
Plaque presented by the Monmouth County Human Relations Commission for "your courage and conviction." January 2002.
Plaque presented by Bradley Elementary School in Asbury Park "in appreciation for his fine character." March 2001.

Gustavo Gac-Artigas, Chilean, writer and theater director, is the author of *Ado's Plot of Land* (*El solar de Ado*), *Tiempo de soñar*, *Un asesinato corriente* and *¡E il orbo era rondo!* (novels).
Dalibá, la brujita del Caribe (short stories).
Pablo Pueblo, *El país de las lágrimas de sangre o nosotros te llamamos Chile Libertad*, *Gonzalito o ayer supe que puedo volver*, *El huevo de Colón o Coca-Cola les ofrece un viaje de ensueños por América Latina* y *Descubrimentando* (plays).
Exiliadas (poems).

Dr. Priscilla Gac-Artigas, Puerto Rican, a specialist in Latin American literature, is the Chair of the Department of Foreign Language Studies at Monmouth University, NJ.
She has published *Melina, conversaciones con el ser que serás* (memoir), two reference books for the teaching of Spanish and French, and many critical essays on Latin American women writers.
Editor of the critical anthology *Reflexiones, ensayos sobre escritoras hispanoamericanas contemporáneas,*(2 Vols.) published in the USA and in Spain.
Translator of *Yo, Alejandro, my/our Story* (English to Spanish) and of *El solar de Ado* (*Ado's Plot of Land*) from Spanish to English.

www.ingramcontent.com/pod-product-compliance
Lightning Source LLC
Chambersburg PA
CBHW020006050426
42450CB00005B/333